AN EASTER BIBLE VERSE TO R[

A WONDERFUL
SURPRISE

SALLY MICHAEL

Illustrated by SENGSAVANE CHOUNRAMANY

Dedicated to Everest Rand Pederson.
May Jesus be your Savior and King.

New Growth Press, Greensboro, NC 27401

Text Copyright © 2025 by Sally Michael

Illustration Copyright © 2025 by Sengsavane Chounramany

Cover/Interior illustrations: Sengsavane Chounramany
Art Direction and Typesetting: Dan Stelzer

ISBN: 978-1-64507-497-7 (paperback)
ISBN: 978-1-64507-498-4 (ebook)

Library of Congress Control Number: 2024946846

Printed in India

32 31 30 29 28 27 26 25   1 2 3 4 5

BLESSED IS THE KING WHO COMES IN THE NAME OF THE LORD!

LUKE 19:38a

What do you say when you are really excited,
or when you think something is really great?

Maybe you say, "Hooray!" or "Wow!"

The Bible tells about a crowd of people who were excited. They weren't just a little excited. They were a LOT excited! But they didn't yell, "Hooray!" or "Wow!"

They shouted, "Hosanna!"

And they shouted, "BLESSED IS THE KING WHO COMES IN THE NAME OF THE LORD!"

What was so exciting? Who were they shouting about?

The crowd was excited about Jesus! Jesus was coming!
Jesus was riding into the city on a donkey!
The people were so happy that they threw leafy branches on the road.
They took off their coats and threw them down for Jesus to ride over.

The people were excited that God had sent them a King.

They yelled over and over,

"HOSANNA! BLESSED IS THE KING WHO COMES IN THE NAME OF THE LORD!"

But Jesus knew something about these people.
He knew most of them really did not love him or want
him to be their true King. He knew that soon they
would be shouting something very different.

Jesus was right. A few days later the people were shouting, "Crucify him!" "Hang him on a cross!"

The people wanted Jesus to die. They were no longer shouting, "Blessed is the King who comes in the name of the Lord!"

They did not love Jesus.
They did not believe that he was God's Son.

The angry people hit Jesus.
They made fun of him. They made
a crown of prickly, sharp thorns
and put it on his head.

A crown of thorns is not a king's crown.

Was Jesus really the King who had
come in the name of the Lord?

Then they nailed
Jesus to a cross.

Many people were glad about this.

Others were sad.

Some didn't know what to think.

Jesus's friends were sad and confused.

Wasn't Jesus the King who had come in the name of the Lord?
If he was the King sent by God, why was he on the cross being killed?
Couldn't Jesus have stopped the people from hurting him?

What do you think?

Jesus is God. He can do anything.
He surely could have stopped the people!
But he didn't. Why didn't he?

Jesus, the King of the whole world isn't like other kings.

Jesus came to serve or help others. Jesus came to die for sinners.
He came to save sinners from the punishment for sin.
Jesus came so that we can be friends with God.

So Jesus stayed on the cross, and he died.

After Jesus died, his friends put his body in a tomb,
which looked like a cave. A big stone was rolled
in front of the tomb opening. Soldiers guarded it.

It was a sad day. No one was saying,
"Blessed is the King who comes in the name of the Lord."

But Jesus is stronger than rocks and soldiers.
And Jesus is stronger than sin and death.

Nothing can stop King Jesus!

"BLESSED IS THE KING WHO COMES
IN THE NAME OF THE LORD!"

On the third day,
early in the morning, some of
Jesus's friends went to the tomb.

There they found a
BIG surprise!

The stone was rolled away, and the tomb was open!
Jesus's body wasn't there!
But an angel was sitting in the tomb.
What was going on? What happened to Jesus?

The angel told the women
about an even **BIGGER** surprise.

"Jesus isn't here!" the angel said. "He is alive again!
He has risen from the dead just like he said he would!"
They were so excited! They ran to tell others the news,
"Jesus is alive! Jesus is alive!"

"BLESSED IS THE KING WHO
COMES IN THE NAME OF THE LORD!"

Jesus, who was alive again, went to see his friends.

But his friends were afraid.
Could this really be Jesus? He showed them
his hands and his feet with the nail marks.
When they saw the marks, they knew he really
was Jesus, God's Son. They were so happy!

Jesus wanted many of his friends to know
he was alive again. He met them by a lake,
on a mountain, on the road, in small groups,
and even in a group of five hundred people.

What a wonderful surprise! Jesus was alive again!

Then Jesus left to
go to heaven.

Do you like surprises? What kind of surprises do you like?

Someday there will be the GREATEST surprise ever!

No one knows when that day will be.

But on that very special day,

Jesus will come back again!

And the whole world will know that he is
the King who comes in the name of the Lord.
He is the King of kings! He is the King of everyone
and everything! What a surprise this will be!

Won't it be wonderful to cheer and shout together,

"HOSANNA! BLESSED IS THE
KING WHO COMES IN THE NAME
OF THE LORD!"

LIVING BY THE WORD

*What can you do to help remember that Jesus
is the King who died and rose again?*

Talk about it. What is Easter Sunday? Why did Jesus have to die
on the cross? What does resurrection mean?

Make a picture with lots of bright colors. Ask someone to write
"Jesus is alive!" on your picture.

Memorize Luke 19:38a: "Blessed is the King who comes in the name
of the Lord!"

Pray this prayer every day: *Teach me your way, O LORD, that I may
walk in your truth; unite my heart to fear your name (Psalm 86:11).*
Pray that you will learn what the Bible says about God and his ways,
that you will obey God's Word, and that God will give you a new heart.

Additional Resources: *The Very Bad News & the Very Good News; The Greatest Treasure!* and
The Greatest Gift! (a Christmas version of *The Greatest Treasure!*) (available at Truth78.org)

Tips for Helping Young Children Memorize Scripture

Memorizing by repetition works well when teaching verses to young children:

1. **Say the reference.** First, clearly pronounce the reference. Then ask the child to repeat the reference. (You may want to explain that a reference is like an address that tells where to find a verse in the Bible.)

2. **Repeat the verse in sections.** Say the passage in several bite-sized sections, repeating each section with the child.

   For example:
   a. Parent: *In the beginning*; Parent and child: *In the beginning*
   b. Parent: *God created*; Parent and child: *God created*
   c. Parent: *the heavens and the earth*; Parent and child: *the heavens and the earth*

3. **Repeat the reference.**

4. **Review the verse** several more times lengthening the sections each time, giving the reference before and after the passage.

5. **Discuss the verse.** After the passage is memorized (usually in 3-4 repetitions), it is good to dissect it. Explain the meaning of unfamiliar words. Rephrase the passage and talk about how the verse applies to life.

Memory Verse Resources:

"Foundation Verse Cards." Verse cards for 2- to 5-year-olds in ESV or NIV. Truth78. https://www.truth78.org/foundation-verses-resources.

"Foundation Verse Coloring Book." Truth78.org

Fighter Verses. App for Apple or Android (includes Foundation Verses)

PARENT NOTE

Children learn about God in baby steps—little steps of learning who he is, what he has done, and what he is doing now, plus little steps of obedience to his teaching and his ways. And, by God's grace, what they learn in little steps of trusting Jesus eventually grows into big steps of faith.

But children don't learn these things by themselves through their natural instincts. They learn them when they are taught the truths of God's Word. In Psalm 86:11, David humbly prays, "Teach me your way, O Lord." The ways of God are contrary to our sinful nature, which is why we must be taught by God (see also Proverbs 14:12 and Isaiah 55:8).

Teaching God's truth is necessary to lead children to obey the Lord from the heart. Children may obey God's commands simply because they like to please their parents or because it's expected of them. This can be a positive step, but it falls short of the kind of obedience that flows from personal conviction and love for God. Such conviction can only be brought about by teaching and the work of the Holy Spirit.

To come to saving faith, a child must embrace the whole of David's prayer in Psalm 86:11: "Teach me your way, O Lord, that I may walk in your truth; unite my heart to fear your name." Notice how he prays that the truth of God would affect his whole heart and life. Real, saving faith requires a change of heart. It requires embracing who God is and entrusting oneself completely to Jesus Christ.

God's Word can make your child "wise for salvation through faith in Christ Jesus" (2 Timothy 3:15). As you use God-breathed Scripture to teach, reprove, correct, and train your child in righteousness (2 Timothy 3:16), the Holy Spirit may chip away at your child's "heart of stone" and turn it into a "heart of flesh" (Ezekiel 36:26). Steps taken when little may lead your child to saving faith—to trusting in Jesus for the forgiveness of sin and the fulfillment of all his promises.

Your part as parent, grandparent, or other discipler of the next generation is to be a teacher, an example of walking in God's ways, and a model of a heart dedicated to God. May your prayer for yourself and your children each day be:

Teach me your way, O Lord,
that I may walk in your truth;
unite my heart to fear your name.
—Psalm 86:11

How to Use This Book

This book will encourage your child to trust Jesus and walk in his ways.
The goal is to instruct their mind, engage their heart, and influence their will.

To Instruct the Mind

- Read the book several times.
- Explain any words or concepts unfamiliar to your child.
- Help your child to memorize the verse.

To Engage the Heart

- Interact with your child as you read the book. Dialogue about God and his ways. Help your child to see God's greatness and goodness. (See *Helping Children to Understand the Gospel* in the resource list.)
- Encourage your child to trust God in everyday events.
- Pray that your child would be receptive to the truth, trust Christ, and walk in his ways.
- Pray with your child that Jesus would give them a heart to love and glorify God.

To Influence the Will

- Talk with your child about ways to apply the verse in real-life situations.
- Encourage your child to act on what they have learned and to practice obedience to the truth.
- Guide your child in walking in the truth and living what they have learned.

Other Resources for Parents:

The Disciple-Making Parent: A Comprehensive Guidebook for Raising Your Children to Love and Follow Jesus by Chap Bettis

Gospel-Powered Parenting: How the Gospel Shapes and Transforms Parenting by William P. Farley

Helping Children to Understand the Gospel by Sally Michael, Jill Nelson, and Bud Burk

Instructing a Child's Heart by Tedd and Margy Tripp

Mothers, Disciplers of the Next Generation by Sally Michael

Reaching Your Child's Heart: A Practical Guide to Faithful Parenting by Juan and Jeanine Sanchez